Ices and Ice Creams

Ices and Ice Creams

Agnes B. Marshall

◧ SQUARE PEG

LONDON

Published by Square Peg 2013
2 4 6 8 10 9 7 5 3 1

Copyright © Square Peg
Text and illustrations © Metropolitan Museum of Art
Introduction © Robin Weir
Design by Dinah Drazin

First published in 1885 as *The Book of Ices*
Introduction and updates by Barbara Ketcham Wheaton 1976

The Random House Group Limited Reg. No. 954009

Addresses for companies within The Random House Group Limited can be found at: www.randomhouse.co.uk

A CIP catalogue record for this book is available from the British Library

ISBN 978 0 22 409560 0

The Random House Group Limited supports the Forest Stewardship Council (FSC®), the leading international forest certification organisation. Our books carrying the FSC® label are printed on FSC®-certified paper. FSC® is the only forest certification scheme endorsed by the leading environmental organisations, including Greenpeace. Our paper procurement policy can be found at www.randomhouse.co.uk/environment

Printed and bound in Germany by GGP Media, GmbH

CONTENTS.

FOREWORD

Had she been alive today, Mrs. Agnes Bertha Marshall would have been judged a formidable force in business.

For a Victorian woman she was truly extraordinary. Much more so than Mrs. Beeton, known by all for her *Book of Household Management*, first published in book form in 1861. For although Mrs. Beeton instructed a then newly emerging middle class on how to conduct themselves and manage servants, her 900 recipes, submitted by readers, were quite often unreliable.

So how come Mrs. Beeton became an icon of Victorian England and not Mrs. Marshall?

For the researcher there is little to be found on Mrs. Marshall's formative years. She seems to leap, fully formed, into the world of cookery in its widest sense.

To describe Agnes as a workaholic is surely no exaggeration. A brisk review of her accomplishments is guaranteed to leave the reader breathless. In 1883 following her purchase of premises in Mortimer Street in London (it was very unusual for women to purchase property, particularly with their own money, a practice only legalized in 1870), Mrs. Marshall opened a cookery school starting with no pupils on the first day. A year later she was demonstrating to classes of up to 40 people, five or six days a week.

In 1885 this *Book of Ices* was published. At first glance a modest little volume, but unique at the time. Prior to this all specialist cookery books had been written by men and only bought by confectioners. Here then was Agnes blithely stepping into a man's world, offering reliable recipes and clear instructions on how to make ices in Victorian homes, thus meeting the needs of an ever increasing middle class of society bent on bettering themselves by dazzling their friends and neighbours with the excellence of their table. Reflect too, that the business of making ices was not straightforward.

Prompt to respond to the commercial opportunities, Mrs. M. offered hand-cranked ice-cream machines to aid the cook which, even today when pitted against modern electric machines, usually prove to be faster and more reliable. The chilling of ingredients was accomplished by surrounding the churn with ice and salt. It is interesting to note that at this time ice was a relative newcomer here in the UK, for in 1901 New York was using 3,000,000 tons, while London only used 450,000 tons.

Once the ice cream was made, again Mrs. Marshall was there to offer splendid moulds in which to form them and 'ice caves' to freeze them solid and preserve them. Prior to this it would have have been necessary to go to a coppersmith for copper moulds and a pewterer for pewter moulds and a cooper to make the buckets. Imagine how much organization it took for Mrs. M. to bring all these trades together under one roof and build a business of this order and magnitude. But this was only a part of her empire.

In 1886, no doubt using the facilities of the cookery school, she launched a weekly magazine called *The Table*, featuring tested recipes, menus, ideas for table settings and seasonal best buys for food. She also used the magazine as a forum to air her own views on the disgraceful quality of some butter, the adulteration of milk, the servant 'problem' and her other, often forthright, views. She was always particularly concerned with the training of cooks and the general standard of cooking. Concurrent with all of this she ran an employment agency for cooks and domestics and would design, supply and install complete kitchens anywhere in the country.

In 1892 she undertook an extensive lecturing tour of major cities in England, taking the stage with a team of helpers to cook an entire meal in front of audiences of up to 600 people. *Fancy Ices* was published in 1894 and took ices to a more elaborate and embellished level. Here she presented to the reader for the first time the concept of the ice-cream cone.

By this time Mrs. M. was supplying not only cookery equipment but also ingredients such as baking powder, Coralline pepper, high-quality extracts, flavours, colours, equipment and ingredients amounting to a range of over 600 products in her catalogue.

Surely the sheer staggering scale of her achievements is un-equalled. Mrs. Marshall was a unique one-woman industry. Her recipes were always concise, accurate, detailed and, what's more, always worked. She was without doubt one of the foremost Victorian cooks and deserves far more credit than she has been given by history. Hopefully this new publication of her first book will make her achievements known to a wider audience.

Robin Weir

INTRODUCTION

by Barbara Ketcham Wheaton

About Agnes B. Marshall

Agnes B. Marshall, with her husband, Alfred William Marshall, operated a cooking school and an employment agency for superior cooks; she had a store which sold kitchen equipment, some of it of her own design; she sold imported and speciality foods, lectured, and published a weekly paper and four cookbooks. *The Book of Ices* was her first. It appeared in 1885, the same year that she introduced her patent ice-cream freezer and 'ice cave' or storage box.

In 1883, she took over the Mortimer Street School of Cookery. By 1885 she was giving lecture demonstrations five or six days a week. Already her shop was offering a wide range of kitchen equipment. She had her name embossed on most of the cast-iron items she sold; similarly, it was pressed into the glass of her bottles of flavourings and colours. The reader of *The Book of Ices* will observe that the contents of these bottles are used lavishly. Agnes Marshall never forgot any of her enterprises for a moment. We may be sure that the gas stove she cooked on was of the same make that was sold in her store. The walls of her classroom bore advertisements for her penny paper, *The Table*, for her leaf gelatine, for *The Book of Ices*. The wooden drums of baking powder she sold contained coupons which could be collected and exchanged for copies of her books. Her later books require the use of recipes available only in the earlier ones, a feature which she puts in a favourable light by pointing out that she thus avoids repetition. All of her cookbooks call for extensive use of her food products and kitchen equipment, and all of them conclude with a section of advertisements showing extracts from her sales catalogues. She offered more than a thousand varieties and sizes of moulds alone; *The Book of Ices* and, later, her *Fancy Ices* must have helped to sell them. The advertisements include descriptions of her school and extensive quotations from favourable press notices, of which there were many.

It is not surprising, then, that the appearance of *The Book of Ices* coincided with the introduction of her patent freezer, and that on page two she recommends that the reader attend a lesson on ices at her school. Ice-cream desserts enjoyed considerable social esteem at the time, because they called for expensive ingredients, special equipment, careful timing, and the attentions of a skilled cook. Often ices were bought, as they are today, rather than made at home.

Among the proliferating cookery schools of the day, Mrs.

Marshall's was distinguished by being predominantly for cooks serving upper-class tables. The National Training School for Cookery, an ancestor of home-economics schools, trained teachers of cooking. Individuals with special skills offered more specialized instruction: an English colonel returned from India gave lessons in curries; 'a French cordon-bleu' had classes for ladies who wished to do French cooking. Mrs. Marshall addressed herself especially to domestics serving in upper-class households; her lectures were attended by female cooks 'and their ladies.' Her notices in the *Times* describe the kind of cookery she taught as 'high-class cookery, French and English.'

While the modern diner may well be puzzled at the state of mind which produces dishes such as vegetable ice cream, a brief consideration of the late-nineteenth-century menu shows how this came about. The formal Victorian dinner was long, lasting two or even three hours, and consisted of many courses. Ices could appear in two or even three of them. The meal was divided into two parts. A soup course came first, followed by three courses: fish, entrée, and relevé or remove. The latter was a large roast garnished with vegetables. The second part of the meal opened with a sorbet or a punch – a water ice flavoured with rum or other spirits – thus contrasting with the hot liquid at the beginning of the meal. Then the diner went on to successive courses of more roast meat, vegetables, and sweets. In her *Cookery Book* Mrs. Marshall describes the character of a sorbet:

Under the term sorbet are now included those ices which are served after the removes. They should be of a light semi-frozen nature, having only just sufficient consistency to hold together when piled up. This degree of solidity is a natural consequence of their composition, for the sugar and spirit among their ingredients, when properly prepared, will prevent them, under any circumstances, becoming as solid as cream and water ices. They are generally prepared by first making an ordinary lemon-water ice, and adding to this some spirit, liqueur, or syrup for flavouring, and fruit for garnish, and are named accordingly rum sorbet, cherry sorbet, and so on. They are always served in cups or glasses, one for each guest, and many very pretty designs are specially made for this purpose.

The coldness and granular texture of the sorbet, the acidity of the lemon juice, and the slight bitterness from the infused lemon peel provide a refreshing contrast to the heat and the unctuous textures of preceding courses. Just how elaborate the 'pretty designs' could be is illustrated by Ranhofer's 'Stanley Punch,' a very liquid sorbet made with coffee, lemons, kirsch, maraschino, and meringue. The punch was served 'inside of a goblet beside which is a heron made of gum paste surrounded by grasses'. Presumably the diner could imagine himself an African explorer foraging for his dinner.

As the Victorian meal drew to a close, the *entremets* course was served. Nowadays this is understood to mean the dessert, but in Mrs.. Marshall's day it included vegetables as well, and even the savoury seems originally to have belonged in it. Each diner chose whatever appealed to him from the selection offered; it was not expected that anyone would want to take helpings of everything. The *entremets* demonstrated by Mrs.. Marshall at an 'Entire Dinner Lesson' at her school in 1892 included a dish of cardoons with beef marrow; small baskets of nougat 'à la Dürer'; *bombe à la portugaise* (a moulded dessert of rum and peach ice, lined with kirsch cream ice, garnished with maidenhair fern and spun sugar); and a savoury (*petites croustades à la Victoria*). In such mixed company a cucumber ice would hardly be out of place.

Mrs. Marshall's enthusiasm warms when she describes the sweets:

> The aim of a properly constructed sweet is to convey to the palate the greatest possible amount of pleasure and taste, whilst it is in no way either suggestive of nourishment or solidity . . . Of late ices and iced dishes of various kinds have increased so much in popular favour as to form a special, and decidedly important item, at every well-arranged dinner . . . At large parties two sorts of ices are usually served, and should be carefully contrasted. A pleasing variety is often produced by filling little moulds with different kinds of ice, which are then served in tiny lace paper cups, under the name of *glacés assorties*, or else the different colours and flavours are placed in the same mould either regularly

or not; in the latter case they produce a marbled effect, suggestive of the Venetian glass known as millefiori or 'colourito'. Another very popular form is the Neapolitan ice, or crème panachée as it is sometimes called, which is produced by filling a metal box, made for the purpose, with layers of differently flavoured and coloured cream and water ices; for instance, lemon, vanilla, chocolate, and pistachio. When moulded these are turned out, cut across in slices, and, served in little paper lace cases, offer the requisite variety to both sight and palate.

The Book of Ices was followed, in 1888, by *Mrs.. A. B. Marshall's Cookery Book*, a long, general-purpose cookbook, of which eventually sixty thousand copies were sold. She interspersed authorship with repeated remodellings of her shop and classrooms, and, in the 1880s, with an ambitious series of lecture tours. Her demonstration lecture 'A Pretty Luncheon' was seen in many of England's principal towns, often under the patronage of titled ladies. These tours brought her favourable notice in the newspapers, an advantage she was quick to exploit. The pinnacle of recognition came when a special London lecture was noticed in the *Times*:

A crowded audience, which filled to its utmost capacity the large banqueting hall of Willis's Rooms [a respectable restaurant near St. James's Palace] assembled on Saturday afternoon to hear Mrs.. A. B. Marshall demonstratively explain several of the operations of high-class cookery, and to watch her prepare many *recherché* dishes, which she classified together under the title 'A Pretty Luncheon.' In a few clear words Mrs.. Marshall explained what she intended to do, and how she proposed to proceed, and for two hours she completely engrossed the earnest attention of some 600 people, instructing and entertaining them at the same time. At the end of the lecture, or performance, whichever it may be called, her labours elicited a unanimous outburst of applause.

A trip to the United States in the summer of 1888 was less successful. She returned without any usable newspaper articles, although she was briefly noticed by the *Philadelphia Evening Bulletin*. The newspaper described Mrs.. Marshall as 'a brunette of fine form and bearing, under middle age, with the ruddy complexion that characterizes English women. She is a fluent talker and speaks with a marked English accent.' She did return with some new recipes to put in her next cookbook, *Mrs.. A. B. Marshall's Larger Cookery Book of Extra Recipes* (1891). In it we find Philadelphia doughnuts and Chicago doughnuts, flannel cakes, Saratoga potato chips, and a recipe for corn on the cob. If she did not succeed in popularizing the last, we need not be surprised. She boiled the corn for an hour, then served it cold, masked with a mayonnaise-like sauce to which were added puréed oysters. This new book was dedicated to Helena, Princess Christian of Schleswig-Holstein, a daughter of Queen Victoria. Mrs.. Marshall had given dinners, 'with vaudeville entertainment', for the poor in the East End of London; Princess Christian also concerned herself with feeding the hungry. Thus it came about that, in the spring of 1888, Mrs.. Marshall gave 'a fully-illustrated practical lecture on high-class cookery' in London, under the patronage of the Princess, 'in aid of the Board School Children's Free Dinner Fund'.

Her career as an entrepreneur and teacher continued until her death in 1905 at the age of fifty. Her husband and the school survived her, the latter continuing on Mortimer Street until the early 1950s.

What is most notable about Agnes Marshall is the way in which she was able to span so many divisions of English society. We may smile at her relentless promotion of her enterprises, but the work she did served the needs of people in many classes. Wealthy hostesses in need of temporary or permanent cooks, middle-class women who wanted to set fashionable tables, ambitious young women in domestic service, Mrs. Marshall served them all.

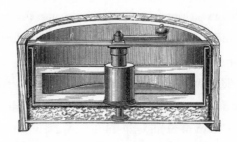

How to Use This Book

Mrs.. Marshall's recipes are practical, and most of them are delicious. No experience is needed, and no great investment in equipment. Making ice cream is not at all like performing magic rituals; there is a great deal of room for experiment and adaptation. *The Book of Ices* may be used in two different ways by the twenty-first-century cook. To taste Victorian flavours, one will follow the recipes exactly. Or, to give variety to a repertory of modern ice creams, the cook may vary them with some of Agnes Marshall's ideas. All kinds of fruit and fruit jams and syrups make good water ices, and many are delicious in the custard and cream ices. Liqueurs, even the more bizarre ones, if discreetly used, can have something to contribute. Different flavours of ice cream combine well with each other. Bombes repay the cook's effort generously, and every household should have its own *bombe maison*. Mrs.. Marshall's are worth considering:

White coffee and strawberry cream
Vanilla cream and strawberry, raspberry, or cherry water
Brown-bread and chocolate creams
Tea cream (*crème de thé*) and burnt-almond cream
Almond and blackcurrant cream (*crème de cassis*)

The textures produced by the recipes in *The Book of Ices* are much more varied than the textures of modern frozen desserts. There are sumptuously smooth custards, slightly grainy frozen creams, and sorbets with the consistency of slushy snow; one learns that things can melt in the mouth in a great variety of ways. The differences in richness are striking, too. The rich, custard-based ice creams exactly fit our modern idea of Victorian food, but we have been led by our preconceptions to overlook the great variety of textures, of tartness, flavours, and combinations which were then and still are possible. The water ices are acid; their flavours are intense. They are as welcome at the end of rich meal as they are unexpected.

One of the many advantages of homemade ice cream is that its degree of richness may be adjusted to the needs of a particular flavour and of a particular meal by selecting the fatness of the cream, or cream and milk mixture, and varying the quantity of egg yolks. The nut ice creams, for example, are made with large amounts of egg yolk; therefore the cook will probably choose to use single (light) cream, or cream and milk, because anything richer would be excessively fat. On the other hand, the richness of a custard made entirely with cream combines very well with coffee or liqueurs. The substantial flavour of chocolate can fill out the lightness of a mixture that contains little or no cream. You may choose to make the fruit ice creams either light or rich according to what has already been served. Peach combines well with single (light) cream, but at the end of a light meal you might choose a custard base instead. Whenever fruit is used it should be entirely ripe, with its flavour fully developed.

The basic cream-ice recipes Agnes Marshall gives us, Numbers 1 through 5, allow the cook a great deal of control over expense, richness, and flavour. It should be noted, though, that even the most expensive ingredients will cost little more than an equivalent amount of high-quality commercial ice cream. Indeed, the simpler cream ices and the water ices will usually cost less to make than they would to buy – if they were obtainable. Mrs.. Marshall's first base custard, 'Very Rich,' is indeed sumptuous and should be used for festive occasions. Number 2, 'Ordinary', is an ideal all-purpose ice-cream base, nearly as rich as the first when it is made with a large proportion of cream, or lighter if only milk is used. The generous quantity of egg yolks in it guarantees a deliciously smooth ice cream. It is especially good with nuts. When made with milk rather than cream, though still good, it does not accord with the Department of Agriculture's definition of ice cream. Neither does 'Common', but the gelatine in it produces a surprisingly agreeable light ice, which is very good in a sugar cone. Number 4, 'Cheap', makes a tasty frozen dessert rather like a milk sherbet; crushed fruit is good with it. Number 5, 'Plain Cream Ice', is like Philadelphia ice cream. It does not, however, contain the dash of salt which gives the latter its unusual quality.

These recipes can be a revelation to the modern palate, jaded as it is with monotonous, artificially flavoured and preserved commercial ice creams. Even the most resolutely modern cook should try some of these recipes in their pure form. Many of the more exotic-sounding ingredients are not very difficult to locate, and there are reasonable substitutes. The techniques are simpler now, because we have so much useful machinery. No longer is the cook obliged to spend hours rubbing fruit through horsehair sieves or through a tammy cloth, or pounding nuts in a mortar. The equipment you already have in your kitchen will be enough. A hand-operated food mill makes splendid purées; the French kind with three interchangeable grids is especially useful, since it allows a choice of textures. If you have a blender you will probably use it for purées, chopping nuts, and making breadcrumbs. The food processor will do all of these things. Occasionally you may still want to run a purée through a sieve to make sure that the blender or processor has left no over-sized lumps. Very small pieces of crushed fruit are good in ice cream; large ones freeze into disagreeable lumps. A discreet quantity of chopped or slivered nuts may be stirred into an ice cream after its initial freezing.

As we have seen, some of Mrs. Marshall's best ice creams are made with custards; the cook who avoids making them because they might curdle is being unnecessarily cautious. In making a 'boiled' custard (which must *not*, in fact, boil), I always insure against curdling by keeping a bowl of cold water next to the stove. Then, if the mixture begins to thicken too quickly, I can stop the cooking immediately by plunging the bottom of the pan into cold water. A curdled custard, however, will do your ice cream very little harm. I deliberately brought a batch of custard (Number 2) to a full boil, and the ice cream made from it was nearly indistinguishable from ice cream made in the usual way. In fact, my advice to the novice custard cook would be to plan to make ice cream regularly, until curdling becomes unthinkable.

In modern ice-cream recipes, some techniques are different. We make them smoother with meringue; fruit is not added until the freezing process is half done. But Mrs. Marshall's recipes would nearly always work as they are written, and it is useful to be reminded that in the kitchen there are often several different ways of achieving satisfactory results. Mrs. Marshall uses food colouring to excess, even putting red food colouring in the cranberry ice, and sometimes she prefers her kirsch and maraschino flavouring syrups to the real kirsch and maraschino which they imitate. The Victorians did like intense and rather heavy colours. Remembering, moreover, that Mrs. Marshall was a persistent saleswoman, we will do as we please.

The modern cook can choose from a variety of freezing equipment. For the soufflés, mousses, and muscovites, which are still-frozen, only a freezer is needed. I have also made ice cream which is meant to be stir-frozen by putting it in a metal bowl in the freezer and stirring the mixture vigorously for one minute every half hour. The resulting ice cream is not so smooth as that made in a crank freezer, but it still tastes better than any that can be bought. I would urge anyone who lacks the storage space for an ice-cream freezer to try this simple alternative.

Homemade ice creams do not have the keeping qualities of the commercial varieties; this is the price we pay for omitting preservatives and chemical compounds. Homemade ice creams are best frozen the day they are to be eaten, although the basic mixture may be made up the day before and kept, well chilled, until it is time to freeze it. The usual tasting a careful cook does must take into account the effect of cold on flavours. Sweetness diminishes as liquids cool, and the balance among flavours alters. An ice-cream mixture that tastes exactly right before it is frozen may be insipid afterwards. Just keep tasting, and you will learn how to adjust flavours to your own liking.

Ice cream lends itself splendidly to decorative presentation. No sensible diner will feel at all cheated by a plain dish of homemade ice cream, 'served rough', as Agnes Marshall puts it. On the other hand, people always like to see an ornamental dessert. Fancy moulds are excellent for decorative effects. Modern aluminium copies of old lead individual moulds can be found; a variety of shapes makes a very pretty sight on the table. Tinned iron moulds sometimes discolour red fruits such as raspberries or strawberries, and no worn tinned copper mould should ever be used, because of the danger of poisoning. Ordinary mixing bowls and loaf pans make perfectly satisfactory substitutes. The larger a mould is, the longer it will take to set firm. Mrs. Marshall's recommended freezing times should be disregarded; each cook will work out timings suitable to his or her own kitchen.

An ice cream made in the morning and moulded in the early afternoon will be quite ready to serve in the evening. To make a bombe, an outer layer of very firm ice cream is pressed into place in a chilled mould with the back of a spoon. The mould is put in the freezer until it is quite firm; then the filling can be pressed into place.

Unmoulding the ice cream need not be an ordeal. If your mould has a flat bottom, it may be lined with a piece of waxed paper cut to shape. The mould, with or without this lining, is quickly dipped in warm – not hot – water, and then dried. A chilled serving plate, with or without a paper doily, is placed over the mould, and both the mould and the plate are inverted. If the ice cream does not slip out easily, the mould and the plate may be shaken gently. If the ice cream is quite firm, it will hold its shape well. Small imperfections may be dealt with by smoothing the ice cream with the side of a knife blade; and there are very few catastrophes which cannot be hidden under whipped cream. Ice cream, once unmoulded onto its plate, can be kept in the freezer for an hour or two. The chilled plate and the paper doily (Mrs. Marshall's 'dish paper') will help prevent skidding: cold ice cream on a room-temperature plate can achieve a remarkable degree of mobility. Pleated paper soufflé cases, which are now sometimes sold as nut cups, and their porcelain replicas may also be used for individual servings. Champagne glasses of the broad, shallow type are excellent for serving sorbets.

Simple decorations can be made quickly; crystallized flowers and mint leaves can be put on in seconds, and whipped cream put through a fluted pastry tube takes very little more time. A sprinkling of chopped nuts is often attractive; the green of pistachio is especially good with whipped cream on any of the strawberry ices.

Nineteenth-century presentations were often very elaborate. Mrs. Marshall's *Fancy Ices* deals with them at great length. Take, for example, the 'Princess Christian Timbale'. A truncated cone of orange cake, hollow in the centre, is covered with a maraschino icing. The centre is filled with alternate layers of pistachio, strawberry, and maraschino ice cream; this ensemble is then set on a base of nougat and sprinkled with pistachio nuts and crystallized rose petals. Whenever such ice-cream-and-cake combinations are made, it is of the utmost importance that the cake be frozen until it is as cold as the ice cream. Then, shortly before serving, it may be moved from the freezer to the refrigerator.

Spun sugar was a favourite nineteenth-century ornament, and Mrs. Marshall's recipe, which follows, is still practical, though half the quantity is more than ample. When the syrup is the colour of light honey it will spin readily. A fork with widely spaced tines works well. If the sugar is spun very fine it will be delicate and pliable, but when thickly spun it is like needles and can inflict a painful cut. Practise until you can spin it fine; discard any that is not. It is easier to spin sugar on a dry day, because sugar is very sensitive to damp and will not spin so well in a humid room. Spun sugar must be made within a few hours of use, and kept in a very dry place. Once spun, it can be cut with scissors. Swathed around a moulded ice it makes a handsome silvery wreath.

> Put half a pound [225ml/1 cup] of water and one pound [450ml/2¼ cups] of Marshall's Cane Sugar [caster/granulated] into a clean copper sugar boiler or thick stewpan, cover the pan over, bring the contents to the boil, remove any scum as it rises from time to time, and continue boiling until the liquid forms a thick bubbled appearance (commonly called the crack); then take a small portion on a clean knife or spoon and plunge it immediately into cold water, and if it is then quite brittle and leaves the knife or spoon quite clear it is ready for spinning. If it clings or is at all soft or pliable continue the boiling until as above. When ready, take a small portion on a fork or spoon and rapidly throw it to and fro over a slightly-oiled rolling pin; continue until sufficient threads of sugar are obtained.

The use, with Mrs. Marshall's 'American' sorbet, of imitation glasses made of frozen ice water, is an attractive conceit. Why American? These sorbet glasses were first used in the United States. A variety of ices in frozen containers was described by Ranhofer in *The Epicurean*. Among the celebrated visitors to New York to be honoured by a banquet at Delmonico's was Charles Dickens. The gargantuan meal served him in 1867 had a *sorbet à l'américaine* for its mid-dinner respite. Ranhofer's recipe for it describes the use of glasses of ice, made from two-piece moulds. In them he serves a lemon and orange sorbet enhanced with American champagne, kirsch, and prunelle. Dishes that self-destruct are a labour-saving device we should invent again. Mrs. Marshall gives further information about these ice cups:

> The sorbet à l'américaine is peculiarly interesting, as it was first served in the cups or glasses formed of raw ice prepared in moulds in imitation of wine-glasses or cups. Its flavouring, when prepared in New York, is the sparkling Californian wine, Catawba, for which champagne is generally substituted in Europe. The moulds for making these ice-cups or glasses consist of two parts, an inner and an outer cup, so that when fixed together they have the appearance of one cup; but between the two parts is a space which is filled with pure or coloured water. These are set in the ice-cave till the water is frozen; the ice-cups are then turned out of the moulds and used. The pretty effects which can be produced by real ice-glasses prepared in this way are so numerous that these moulds are now being used for sorbets of any kind.

More than half of the recipes in *The Book of Ices* have been tested, including examples of all the basic kinds and all the more improbable ones. The recipes were followed exactly whenever possible. The reader will see that I have reduced the number of egg yolks called for. This is because our eggs are larger. Generally speaking, my family and friends who resolutely tasted their way through more than sixty-five varieties of ice cream were enthusiastic as well as open-minded. The only varieties that no one liked were the curried soufflés à la Ripon, and the spinach cream ice. Of the latter, my son said that it was not bad, but he would rather not eat an entire teaspoonful. The rice cream ice led to argument; whether people liked it or not depended on childhood attitudes to rice pudding. It did have a rather flannelly texture. Reactions to the cucumber ice were strong and diverse. Two people who described themselves as not liking ice cream were pleased by it; the improving effect of a little chopped fresh mint was suggested. There was also disagreement about the brown-bread cream ice; it would do well, I think, as a lining for a bombe. When these curiosities are set aside, the picture becomes more uniform. The strawberry and vanilla bombe and the ginger bombe were especially well liked; so were the Nesselrode pudding and the coffee mousse, to which I added a little cognac. The white coffee cream ice, made with the 'Very Rich' custard base, was wonderful. So, in a quite different way, were the ices. I think that our lemons, like our eggs, may be larger than Mrs.. Marshall's were, because the lemon water ice, when made with six lemons, was really very intense; one diner compared eating it to licking a styptic pencil. When made with four lemons it was delicious. The orange ice was perfect; it bears no resemblance to commercial ices, being fresh and intense and not too sweet. The apple, pear, and cranberry ices were very good. The elderflower was pleasant, if odd; all the strawberry ices and ice creams were wonderful – the plain ice, the mousse, the sorbet, and the plombière – and each had its own special character. The tea mousse was thought insipid. Really strong coffee must be used in making the coffee mousse and soufflé.

Even the simplest mixtures, the plain cream ice and water ice flavoured with fruit syrup, were good. When made with some home-bottled blackberry syrup from a friend's garden, they were delicious. Even commercial syrup, of good quality and with real flavourings, yielded water ices that children ate almost as quickly as they could be made.

The question of how much each recipe yields is difficult to answer because it depends how much air is beaten into the mixture as it freezes. In general, I found that basic ice waters and creams yielded about one litre [one quart] when frozen. When crushed fruit or other bulky ingredients were added, the quantity was proportionally larger. The cook should feel entirely free to double or halve any of these recipes to suit the needs of a particular occasion.

In some of the recipes based on custard (Numbers 1–4), there is an anomaly: 570ml (2½ cups) of custard is called for, although in practice the base recipes begin with 570ml of liquid, to which other ingredients are subsequently added. In testing these recipes, I used the full quantity produced from the recipes as written, and the results were entirely satisfactory.

A Word About Measurements

THESE conversions are approximate. Precise measures were little used in the late-nineteenth-century kitchen. Mrs.. Marshall's 'glasses' may mean anything she wants them to. Sources contemporary with her speak of a sherry wineglass as measuring one ounce, and the port wineglass as containing five ounces. *Whitaker's Almanack* (1894) says a wineglass measures two ounces. In the absence of any guidance from Mrs.. Marshall, use a glass suitable to the liquid being measured: a liqueur glass for kirsch, a sherry glass for sherry, and so forth.

B. K. W.

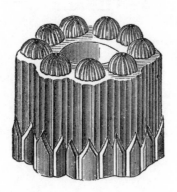

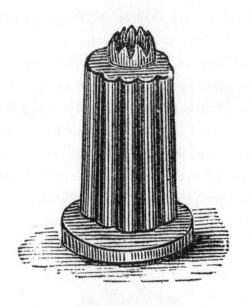

HINTS ON MAKING ICES

1. Too much sugar will prevent the ice from freezing properly.

2. Too little sugar will cause the ice to freeze hard and rocky.

3. If the ices are to be moulded, freeze them in the freezer to the consistency of a thick batter before putting them in the moulds.

4. If they are to be served unmoulded, freeze them drier and firmer.

5. Broken ice alone is not sufficient to freeze or mould the ices; 8 parts rough ice to 1 part rock salt must be used.

6. Fruit ices will require to be coloured according to the fruit.

7. When dishing up ices, whether in a pile or moulded, it will be found advantageous to dish them up on a napkin, as that will not conduct the heat to the bottom of them so quickly as the dish would.

MOULDING AND KEEPING ICES.

Fill your mould with the frozen cream from the freezer, and see
that it is well pressed or shaken into the mould. Place the mould
for 1½ to 2 hours in the freezer; examine from time to time if
you wish. When you desire to turn the ice out of the mould, dip
the mould for an instant in cold water and turn it out as you
would a jelly. If you put the ice, when turned out, back into the
freezer and shut the door, it will keep its shape for many hours,
so that ices can be prepared long before actually required; they
have thus been kept from one day to another.

ICE MOULDS AND MOULDING.

These are to be had in almost endless variety. In using ice
moulds, great taste and novelty can be exercised in dishing up,
and they afford to the cook the opportunity of making some of
the prettiest dishes it is possible to send to the table.

CUSTARDS FOR CREAM ICES

Never allow the *custard to boil*, or it will curdle.

Always add the flavouring when the custard is cooled, unless otherwise stated.

1. Very Rich

570ml (2½ cups) single (light) cream
115g (½ cup) caster (granulated) sugar
7 egg yolks
¼ tsp vanilla essence
285g (1¼ cups) whipped cream (175ml / ¾ cup unwhipped),
optional

Put the cream in a pan over the fire, and let it come to the boil. Allow to cool slightly and then pour it on to the sugar and yolks in a basin and mix well. Return it to the pan and keep it stirred over the fire till it thickens and clings well to the spoon, but do not let it boil; then pass it through a tammy, or hair sieve, or strainer. Let it cool; add vanilla or other flavour, and freeze. Mould if desired. When partly frozen, slightly sweetened whipped cream may be added.

2. Ordinary

570ml (2½ cups) milk or milk and single (light) cream
115g (½ cup) caster (granulated) sugar
7 egg yolks

Prepare this as in the above recipe. Flavour and freeze. This can be improved by using half milk and half cream instead of all milk.

3. Common

570ml (2½ cups) milk
115g (½ cup) caster (granulated) sugar
2 eggs, well beaten
1 tsp (½ tbsp) powdered gelatine, soaked for 5 minutes in
50ml (¼ cup) cold milk

Put these in a pan and stir over the fire to *nearly* boiling. Remove it from the fire and stir in the gelatine. When the gelatine is dissolved, pass it through the tammy, or hair sieve, or strainer. Flavour and freeze as above.

4. Cheap

570ml (2½ cups) milk
115g (½ cup) caster (granulated) sugar
2½ tsp cornflour (corn starch) or arrowroot

Boil the cornflour (corn starch) in the milk with the sugar. Finish as for the other custards.

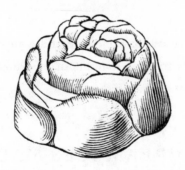

CREAM ICES

5. PLAIN CREAM ICE
(*Crème Glacée*)

570ml (2½ cups) single (light) cream
115g (½ cup) caster (granulated) sugar

Mix and freeze dry.

This can be served in the centre of a compote of fruits, or with fresh fruits arranged round it; or the fruits and the cream can be served on separate dishes.

6. CREAM ICES MADE FROM JAMS

As jams vary exceedingly in the amount of sugar they contain, it is most necessary that this be taken into consideration to ensure success. The following recipe is for jams of average sweetness.

570ml (2½ cups) milk
7 egg yolks
150g (½ cup plus 2 tbsp) jam
285g (1¼ cups) whipped cream (175ml / ¾ cup unwhipped)
sweetened with ½ tsp caster (granulated) sugar
food colouring to match fruit

Boil the milk and allow it to cool slightly, then mix it into 7 raw yolks of eggs, put this in a pan and stir over the fire until it thickens, then add the jam and pass through the tammy or hair sieve. When cool freeze, and when partly frozen add the sweetened whipped cream. Colour the custard with a little red, green, or yellow colour according to fruit.

7. Another way

150g (½ cup plus 2 tbsp) jam
juice of 1 lemon
570ml (2½ cups) single (light) cream

Take the jam as above, and the juice of 1 lemon and the cream; pass through the tammy or sieve, and freeze. Colour according to fruit.

8. CREAM ICES MADE FROM FRUIT AND LIQUEUR SYRUPS

The syrups made by different manufacturers vary much in strength.

285ml (1¼ cups) unsweetened custard (Nos. 1–4)
4 tbsp (⅓ cup) fruit syrup

Make a custard as in Nos. 1, 2, 3, or 4, without sugar, and add syrup to it, and freeze. Mould or serve in a pile.

9. Another way: very simple

4 tbsp (⅓ cup) fruit syrup
285ml (1¼ cups) single (light) cream or milk

Add fruit or liqueur syrup to cream or milk. Freeze. Mould or serve in a pile.

CREAM ICES MADE FROM RIPE FRUITS, ETC

10. Almond or Orgeat Cream Ice
(*Crème d'Amandes*°)

° The French names can be written in either of the following forms, as for Vanilla Cream Ice: Crème à la Vanille, Crème de Vanille and the word 'glacée' may be added; or Glace à la Vanille.

225g (½lb) almonds
3 or 4 drops bitter-almond flavouring or ¼ tsp almond essence
1 tsp orange flower water
570ml (2½ cups) tepid milk or single (light) cream
(or half of each)
115g (½ cup) caster (granulated) sugar
570ml (2½ cups) custard (Nos. 1–4) or
sweetened cream (No. 5)

Blanch, peel, and pound the almonds. During the pounding add a teaspoonful of orange flower water and the essence of almonds, and the tepid milk or cream (or half milk and half cream). Sweeten with the sugar, and add to the custard or sweetened cream. Freeze and serve in a pile on a napkin or mould it.

11. Apple Cream Ice
(*Crème de Pommes*)

900g (2lb) apples
285ml (1¼ cups) water
1-cm (½-in) cinnamon stick
peel of ½ lemon
juice of 1 lemon
170g (¾ cup) sugar
570ml (2½ cups) custard (Nos. 1–4) or
sweetened cream (No. 5)

Peel and cut the apples, put them on the stove in the water with a little piece of cinnamon, the peel of half a lemon, the juice of one, and the sugar. Cook quickly until reduced to a purée, then pass through a tammy cloth or hair sieve (or blend), and mix it with the sweetened cream or custard. Freeze and serve as for previous recipe.

12. Apricot Cream Ice
(*Crème d'Abricots*)

12 apricots, cracked (see page 114)
280ml (1¼ cups) water
115g (½ cup) caster (granulated) sugar
¼ tsp yellow food colouring
½ tsp vanilla essence
850ml (3¾ cups) custard (Nos. 1–4, increased by half) or
cream (No. 5, increased by half)

Cut the apricots in halves, crack the stones and take out the kernels, and put them to cook with the water and sugar. When tender mix a little yellow colouring with the fruit and a few drops of vanilla, and pass through the tammy cloth or hair sieve. Add this purée to the custard or sweetened cream. Freeze and finish as for previous recipes.

13. Banana Cream Ice
(*Crème de Bananes*)

6 ripe bananas

juice of 2 lemons

2 tbsp curaçao

570ml (2½ cups) cream (No. 5) or custard (Nos. 1–4)

Peel the bananas and pound them to a pulp, add the juice of the lemons and the curaçao. Pass through a tammy cloth and finish with the sweetened cream or custard as in the previous recipe.

14. Biscuit Cream Ice
(*Biscuits glacés à la Crème*)

500g (2½ cups) plain biscuit crumbs

This ice can be made with the pieces of any kind of biscuit; rub them through the wire sieve and finish as for brown bread ice (No. 16).

15. Blackcurrant Cream Ice
(*Crème de Cassis*)

450g (1lb) blackcurrants
170g (¾ cup) caster (granulated) sugar
285ml (1¼ cups) water
red food colouring
570ml (2½ cups) custard (Nos. 1–4) or cream (No. 5)
1 tsp lemon juice

Put the blackcurrants, caster sugar, water, and a few drops of red food colouring in a pan, and let them just come to the boil. Pass through the tammy and add the custard or sweetened cream, and lemon juice. Freeze and finish as No. 10.

16. Brown Bread Ice
(*Crème de Pain Bis*)

375g (2½ cups) brown breadcrumbs
160ml (a scant ⅔ cup) crème de noyeau or maraschino syrup
570ml (2½ cups) single (light) cream or milk

Mix the breadcrumbs with the noyeau or maraschino syrup and the cream or milk, and freeze dry. Serve in a pile or mould. This is a good *entremets* or dessert ice, and is much liked for garden and evening parties.

17. Burnt Almond Cream Ice
(*Crème de Pralines*)

225g (½lb) almonds
30g (2 tbsp) butter
30g (2 tbsp) caster (granulated) sugar
570ml (2½ cups) hot milk or single (light) cream sweetened
with 75g (⅓ cup) caster (granulated) sugar
3–4 drops (⅛ tsp) almond essence

Blanch and peel the almonds as in No. 10; put them in a sauté pan with the butter and caster sugar, and fry till a dark brown colour. Then pound in the mortar till smooth, adding by degrees the hot milk or sweetened cream, and 3 or 4 drops of essence of almonds. Pass through the tammy or hair sieve. Freeze and finish as in No. 10.

18. Cedrat Cream Ice
(*Crème à la Cédrat*)

1–2 citron fruit
4–5 lumps sugar
1l (5 cups) lemon cream ice (No. 36)

Take one or two citron and rub them well with 4 or 5 large lumps of sugar, and add these lumps to a litre (quart) of lemon cream ice, and freeze. Serve rough or mould.

19. Cherry Cream Ice
(*Crème de Cerises*)

450g (1lb) cherries
285ml (1¼ cups) water
⅛ tsp almond extract or 3 drops bitter-almond flavouring
75g (⅓ cup) caster (granulated) sugar
juice of 1½ lemons
red food colouring
570ml (2½ cups) custard (Nos. 1–4) or cream (No. 5)
2 tbsp kirsch

Stone the cherries, break the stones and take out the kernels, and cook the cherries and kernels for about 10 minutes in the water and caster sugar; then pound them, and add the juice of 1½ lemons, and a little red food colouring to colour. Pass through a tammy cloth or hair sieve, and add to the custard or sweetened cream and kirsch, and freeze. Serve in a pile on a napkin or mould.

20. Chestnut Cream Ice
(*Crème de Marrons*)

700g (1½lb) chestnuts
½ tsp vanilla essence
75g (⅓ cup) caster (granulated) sugar
570ml (2½ cups) tepid single (light) cream
red food colouring
570ml (2½ cups) custard (Nos. 1–4)
or cream (No. 5), optional

Roast the chestnuts, and when fully softened remove all husk and skin and pound them in a mortar, adding during the pounding by degrees a few drops of essence of vanilla, caster sugar, tepid cream, and 6 drops of red food colouring. When well mixed pass through hair sieve or tammy cloth. This may be frozen as it is, or added to a pint of custard (Nos. 1 to 4) or sweetened cream (No. 5), and finished as in previous recipes.

21. Chocolate Cream Ice
(*Crème de Chocolat*)

110g (4oz) plain (semisweet) chocolate
150ml (½ cup plus 2 tbsp) milk or cold water
570ml (2½ cups) custard (Nos. 1–4) or cream (No. 5)
1 tbsp cocoa powder, optional

Cut the chocolate very fine, and put it in the milk or cold water on the stove to cook till quite dissolved; then add this to the custard or sweetened cream. Freeze and finish as for vanilla cream ice (No. 58).

Cocoa cream ice may be made by adding soluble cocoa to the custard, and finishing as usual.

22. Cinnamon Cream Ice
(*Crème de Cannelle*)

570ml (2½ cups) milk or single (light) cream
2-cm (¾-in) cinnamon stick

1 bay leaf
peel of ½ lemon
7 egg yolks
115g (½ cup) caster (granulated) sugar
yellow food colouring

Put the milk or cream to boil with a piece of cinnamon, a bay leaf, and the peel of half a lemon; when well flavoured, mix it on to 7 raw yolks of eggs and the caster sugar; thicken over the fire. Add a little apricot yellow; tammy, and finish as for other ices.

23. Coconut Cream Ice
(*Crème de Noix de Coco*)

1 coconut
1l (5 cups) custard (Nos. 1–4, doubled)

Grate a small coconut, and stir this with custard just as you take the latter from the fire. Strain through tammy or hair sieve. Freeze and mould as before.

24. Coffee Cream Ice
(*Crème de Café*)

570ml (2½ cups) strong coffee
75g (⅓ cup) caster (granulated) sugar
1l (5 cups) custard (Nos. 1–4, doubled)

Make strong coffee (coffee extract is sometimes used), sweeten with sugar; add this to custard. Freeze and finish as above. This ice will be brown, and not so delicate as the following.

25. White Coffee Cream Ice: very delicate
(*Crème de Café blanche*)

110g (4oz) mocha beans
570ml (2½ cups) single (light) cream
or milk
75g (⅓ cup) sugar
260g (1 cup plus 2 tbsp) whipped cream
(150ml / ½ cup plus 2 tbsp unwhipped)

Take fresh roasted mocha coffee berries, and add them to the cream or milk; let them stand on the stove for an hour, but do not let them boil; strain through a tammy; sweeten with the sugar. Freeze, adding whipped cream during the freezing as for vanilla cream ice (No. 58).

26. Cranberry Cream Ice
(*Crème de Cranberges*)

450g (1lb) cranberries
170g (¾ cup) sugar
red food colouring
285ml (1¼ cups) water
570ml (2½ cups) cream (No. 5)
or custard (Nos. 1–4)
1 tbsp maraschino

Put the cranberries in a pan with the sugar, a few drops of red food colouring, and water. Cook until a pulp, then pass through the tammy, and add sweetened cream or custard, and the maraschino. Freeze and finish as for previous ices.

27. Cucumber Cream Ice
(*Crème de Concombres*)

1 large cucumber
115g (½ cup) caster (granulated) sugar

285ml (1¼ cups) water
2 tbsp ginger brandy
green food colouring
juice of 2 lemons
570ml (2½ cups) cream (No. 5) or custard (Nos. 1–4)

Peel and remove the seeds from the cucumber, and add the sugar and water; cook till tender. Then pound and add to it the ginger brandy and a little green colouring and the juice of 2 lemons; pass through the tammy, and add this to the sweetened cream or custard. Freeze and finish as usual.

28. Curaçoa Cream Ice
(*Crème au Curaçoa*)

570ml (2½ cups) unsweetened custard (Nos. 1–4) or
unsweetened cream (No. 5)
juice of 2 sweet oranges
60ml (¼ cup) curaçoa or curaçao syrup
3 tbsp caster (granulated) sugar

Take the unsweetened custard (Nos. 1 to 4) or unsweetened cream; add the juice of 2 sweet oranges, the curaçoa or curaçoa syrup, and the caster sugar. Freeze and mould or serve roughly.

29. Damson Cream Ice
(*Crème de Prunes de Damas*)

450g (1lb) damson plums
170g (¾ cup) sugar
285ml (1¼ cups) water
red food colouring
570ml (2½ cups) custard (Nos. 1–4) or cream (No. 5)
1 tbsp crème de noyeau

Put the ripe damsons to cook with the caster sugar, the water, and a little liquid red food colouring; just boil up and then pass through the tammy. Add this to the custard or cream, and the noyeau, and freeze.

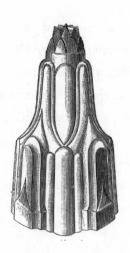

30. Filbert Cream Ice
(*Crème d' Avelines*)

400g (2½ cups) hazelnuts (filberts)
cold water, to cover
7 egg yolks
570ml (2½ cups) single (light) cream
115g (½ cup) caster (granulated) sugar
1 tsp vanilla essence

Shell and put the filberts in a pan with cold water, and put to boil; when they boil strain off and wash in cold water and rub them in a cloth to take off the skins. When this is done, put the filberts in the mortar and pound them till quite smooth; then mix with them gently 7 raw yolks of eggs, the cream, and caster sugar; put it into a pan and stir over the fire to thicken, keeping it stirred all the time; then pass through the tammy, and add a teaspoonful of essence of vanilla, and freeze.

31. Ginger Cream Ice
(*Crème au Gingembre*)

225g (½lb) preserved ginger
8 egg yolks

75g (⅓ cup) caster (granulated) sugar
850ml (3¾ cups) single (light) cream
60ml (¼ cup) ginger wine

Pound the preserved ginger till smooth; then add to it 8 raw yolks of eggs, the sugar, cream, and ginger wine; thicken it over the fire, then tammy and freeze.

32. Gooseberry Cream Ice
(*Crème de Groseilles Vertes*)

750g (5 cups) gooseberries
285ml (1¼ cups) water
170g (¾ cup) sugar
green or red food colouring
570ml (2½ cups) sweetened cream (No. 5)
or custard (Nos. 1–4)

Put the gooseberries on the stove in a pan, with the water and sugar; boil, and when cooked pass through the tammy. If green berries, use a little sap green, or apple green, to colour; if red, a little red food colouring or cherry red. When tammied, mix with the sweetened cream or custard, and freeze.

33. Greengage Cream Ice
(*Crème de Prunes de Reine-Claude*)

900g (2lb) ripe greengage plums
285ml (1¼ cups) water
280g (1¼ cups) sugar
green food colouring
2 tbsp maraschino
1l (5 cups) custard (Nos. 1–4, doubled)
or cream (No. 5, doubled)

Stone the greengages, put the water in a pan with the sugar, and boil the fruit till quite smooth; then add a little green colouring, maraschino, and pass through the tammy. Add this to the custard or cream, and finish as usual.

34. Italian Cream Ice
(*Crème à l'Italienne*)

850ml (3¾ cups) single (light) cream or milk
peel of ¼ lemon
2.5-cm (1-in) cinnamon stick
8 egg yolks

170g (¾ cup) sugar
2 tbsp brandy
1 tbsp crème de noyeau
juice of 1 lemon

Scald the cream or milk, with a little lemon peel and cinnamon, let it cool a little and mix it on to the raw yolks of eggs; sweeten with the caster sugar; thicken over the fire, tammy, and flavour, when cool, with pale brandy, noyeau, and the juice of 1 lemon. Freeze, and serve as in previous recipes.

35. Kirsch Cream Ice
(*Crème au Kirsch*)

850ml (3¾ cups) cream (No. 5, increased by half) or custard
(Nos. 1–4, increased by half)
80ml (⅓ cup) kirsch
2 tbsp brandy
juice of 1 orange or lemon

To the sweetened cream or custard add the kirsch, pale brandy, and the juice of 1 orange or lemon. Freeze.

36. Lemon Cream Ice
(*Crème de Citron*)

peel of 4 to 6 lemons
725ml (3 cups plus 2 tbsp) single (light) cream or milk
150g (⅔ cup) caster (granulated) sugar
8 egg yolks
juice of 4 to 6 lemons

Peel the lemons very thinly, and put this peel to boil, with the cream or milk and the sugar, for 10 minutes; let cool slightly, then mix on to the raw yolks of eggs, and thicken over the fire and pass through the tammy. When cool add the juice from the lemons, which must be strained, and freeze.

37. Marmalade, Orange or Lemon, Cream Ice
(*Crème au Marmelade*)

150g (½ cup plus 2 tbsp) marmalade
570ml (2½ cups) cream or unsweetened custard (Nos. 1–4)
juice of 2 lemons or oranges
2 tbsp orange or lemon syrup

Mix the marmalade with the cream or unsweetened custard and the juice of 2 of the fruit, either lemon or orange, and the orange or lemon syrup. Pass through the tammy, and freeze.

38. Maraschino Cream Ice
(*Crème au Marasquin*)

570ml (2½ cups) cream (No. 5) or
unsweetened custard (Nos. 1–4)
125ml (½ cup) maraschino
juice of 1 lemon

To the cream or unsweetened custard add the maraschino (or maraschino syrup) and the juice of 1 lemon, and freeze.

39. Neapolitan or Pinachée Cream Ices
(*Petites Crèmes à la Napolitaine*)

Panachée: In variegated colours.

Note: A small straight-sided loaf pan can be used for the Neapolitan box.

You must have a Neapolitan box for this ice, and fill it up in 3 or 4 layers with different coloured and flavoured ice creams (a water ice may be used with the custards); for instance, lemon, vanilla, chocolate, and pistachio. Mould for about 1½ to 2 hours, turn it out, cut it in slices, and arrange neatly on the dish on a napkin or dish-paper.

40. Noyeau Cream Ice
(*Crème au Noyeau*)

570ml (2½ cups) single (light) cream
120ml (½ cup) crème de noyeau
juice of 1 orange
juice of 1 lemon

To the cream add the noyeau (or noyeau syrup), and the juice of 1 orange and 1 lemon. Freeze.

41. Orange Cream Ice
(*Crème à l'Orange*)

This is made as for lemon cream ice (No. 36), using oranges instead of lemons.

42. Orange Flower Water Cream Ice
(*Crème à la Fleur d'Oranger*)

110g (4oz) sweet almonds
3 or 4 drops bitter-almond flavouring or ⅛ tsp almond extract
150ml (½ cup plus 2 tbsp) single (light) cream
170g (¾ cup) caster (granulated) sugar
6 egg yolks
570ml (2½ cups) single (light) cream
60ml (¼ cup) orange-flower water
¼ tsp vanilla essence

Blanch the sweet almonds; pound them in the mortar till quite smooth, then mix with the 150ml (½ cup plus 2 tbsp) cream, caster sugar, and raw yolks of eggs; add, when this is mixed well, the rest of the cream, and then thicken over the fire, and tammy. When cool, add the orange-flower water, and a few drops of essence of vanilla, and freeze.

43. Peach Cream Ice
(*Crème de Pêches*)

This is made in the same manner as the apricot cream ice (No. 12). A *very* little red food colouring is used for the colour.

44. Pear Cream Ice
(*Crème de Poires*)

This is made in the same manner as the apple cream ice (No. 11).

45. Pineapple Cream Ice
(*Crème d'Ananas*)

1 pineapple
570ml (2½ cups) water

280g (1¼ cups) caster (granulated) sugar
570ml (2½ cups) cream (No. 5) or custard (Nos. 1–4)
yellow and green food colouring

Peel off the outside of the pineapple; if not fully ripe, it will require to be boiled. Put the pineapple in a clean pan with the water and sugar, and cook till tender. Then pound, and pass through a hair sieve or tammy. To 275ml (1 cup plus 2 tbsp) of this purée add the cream or custard. Freeze. Colour the ice required for the body of the pineapple mould with apricot yellow, and that for the top with a little apple green. Another way is to make a purée of tinned pineapple, and add it to the custard or cream.

46. Pistachio Cream Ice
(*Crème de Pistaches*)

110g (4oz) pistachios
2 tbsp orange-flower water
12 drops vanilla essence
570ml (2½ cups) custard (Nos. 1–4)
green food colouring

Blanch, peel, and pound the pistachio kernels. Add, when thoroughly pounded, the orange-flower water, and 12 drops vanilla essence; pass through sieve or tammy, and add the custard. Colour with apple green or sap green. Freeze and mould.

47. Plum Cream Ice
(*Crème de Prunes*)

900g (2lb) plums
285ml (1¼ cups) water
280g (1¼ cups) sugar
red food colouring
570ml (2½ cups) cream (No. 5) or custard (Nos. 1–4)
a few drops of almond essence

Put the plums in a pan with the water and sugar and a few drops of red food colouring; cook till smooth, and pass through the tammy. To 275ml (1 cup plus 2 tbsp) of this purée add the cream or custard. A few drops of essence of almonds will improve it. Freeze and mould or serve in a pile.

48. Quince Cream Ice
(*Crème de Coings*)

150g (½ cup plus 2 tbsp) quince jam
juice of 2 oranges
juice of ½ lemon
850ml (3¾ cups) cream (No. 5, increased
by half) or unsweetened custard (Nos. 1–4,
increased by half)
yellow food colouring
2 tbsp pineapple syrup

Take the quince jam, and add to it the juice of 2 oranges and of half a lemon, the cream or custard (unsweetened), a little apricot yellow to colour and pineapple syrup. Pass through the tammy, and freeze.

49. Raspberry Cream Ice
(*Crème de Framboises*)

450g (1lb) raspberries
170g (¾ cup) sugar
juice of 1 lemon

570ml (2½ cups) custard (Nos. 1–4) or cream (No. 5)
red food colouring

Take the raspberries and sugar, and the juice of 1 lemon; mix with the custard or cream. Tammy, and colour with liquid red food colouring or cherry red. Freeze, and finish as for other ices.

50. Ratafia Cream Ice
(*Crème au Ratafia*)

Ratafia biscuits: See Glossary.
850ml (3¾ cups) milk
8 egg yolks
170g (¾ cup) sugar
1 tbsp crème de noyeau

Bruise the ratafia biscuits in the mortar. Make a custard of the milk, raw yolks, and sugar; and when it thickens, pour it over the bruised biscuits, and pass altogether through the tammy or hair sieve. Add the noyeau, and freeze.

51. Redcurrant Cream Ice
(*Crème de Groseilles*)

Make this as for raspberry cream ice (No. 49).

52. Rhubarb Cream Ice
(*Crème de Rhubarbe*)

Make this as for gooseberry cream ice (No. 32), using good ripe rhubarb.

53. Rice Cream Ice
(*Crème de Riz*)

570ml (2½ cups) milk or single (light) cream
115g (½ cup) caster (granulated) sugar
peel of 1 lemon
3 bay leaves
5-cm (2-in) cinnamon stick
80ml (⅓ cup plus 2 tbsp) ground rice (Cream of Rice)
60ml (¼ cup) cold milk
a few drops of vanilla essence
285g (1¼ cups) whipped cream (175ml / ¾ cup unwhipped)
sweetened with ½ tsp sugar

Put the milk or cream to boil with the caster sugar, the peel of a lemon, bay leaves, and a little cinnamon. Then put the rice cream (*crème de riz*) in a basin, and mix it into a smooth paste with the cold milk, and add the boiled milk, and let the whole simmer for 10 minutes. Pass through the tammy, strainer, or sieve, and when cold add a few drops of essence of vanilla, and freeze. During the freezing add half a pint of slightly sweetened whipped cream. Mould or serve roughly.

54. Spanish Nut Cream Ice
(*Crème de Noisettes*)

400g (2½ cups) hazelnuts, toasted
7 egg yolks
150g (⅔ cup) caster (granulated) sugar
570ml (2½ cups) single (light) cream
1 tbsp crème de noyeau
1 tbsp brandy

Break the hazelnuts and bake the kernels till crisp, then pound them till smooth, and add the raw yolks of the eggs, the caster sugar, and the cream; put in a stew-pan and stir over the fire till it thickens, and then pass through the tammy cloth. When cool, add the noyeau and the brandy. Freeze and mould or serve in glasses.

Spanish Nut Cream Ice
Another way

400g (2½ cups) hazelnuts
75g (¼ cup) sugar
1 tbsp orange-flower water
285ml (1¼ cups) single (light) cream
2 tbsp maraschino or crème de noyeau
570ml (2½ cups) custard or cream (Nos. 1–5)

Put the kernels of the hazelnuts, with the caster sugar and orange-flower water, in a sauté or stew-pan, and toss over a quick fire until the kernels are quite brown; then pound in the mortar, and mix well with the cream, pass through tammy cloth or hair sieve; flavour with maraschino or noyeau. Add this to the prepared custard or cream. Freeze and mould or serve rough.

55. Strawberry Cream Ice
(*Crème de Fraises*)

Make this as raspberry cream (No. 49).

56. Tangarine Cream Ice
(*Crème de Tangarines*)

12 tangerines
570ml (2½ cups) boiling single (light) cream or milk
7 egg yolks
115g (½ cup) caster (granulated) sugar
yellow food colouring
2 tbsp orange-flower water
570ml (2½ cups) cream or custard (Nos. 1–5), optional

Peel 12 tangarine oranges; make a pulp of the insides. Put the peels in the boiling cream or milk, and let it stand on the stove for a quarter of an hour, but do not let it boil; then mix this with the raw yolks and sugar, and stir over the fire till it thickens; now add the orange pulp, colour with apricot yellow, and pass through the tammy or hair sieve; when cool, add the orange-flower water, and freeze. This may be added to sweetened cream or custard before freezing.

57. Tea Cream Ice
(*Crème de Thé*)

150ml (½ cup plus 2 tbsp) strong tea
2 tbsp sugar
570ml (2½ cups) custard or cream (Nos. 1–5)

Prepare very strong tea, sweetened with sugar, and add this to the custard or cream, and finish as for other ices.

58. Vanilla Cream Ice
(*Crème de Vanille*)

570ml (2½ cups) custard (Nos. 1–4) or cream (No. 5)
2 tsp vanilla essence or 1 vanilla pod
260g (1 cup plus 2 tbsp) whipped cream
(150ml / ½ cup plus 2 tbsp unwhipped)

Prepare a custard or take sweetened cream and flavour with vanilla essence. Freeze and mould or serve in glasses. This is much improved by adding, during the freezing, the whipped cream.

To flavour with a vanilla pod cut it in strips, and let it boil with the milk or cream of your custard, keeping the pan covered.

59. Walnut Cream Ice
(*Crème de Noix*)

Make this as for filbert cream ice (No. 30).

60. White Wine Cream Ice
(*Crème au Vin Blanc*)

8 egg yolks
570ml (2½ cups) single (light) cream
115g (½ cup) caster (granulated) sugar
6 tbsp white wine
2 tbsp pineapple syrup
170g (¾ cup) preserved fruit

Prepare a custard (No. 1) with the raw yolks of eggs, cream, and sugar. When cool, add the white wine and pineapple syrup, and freeze. When frozen, mix in finely cut preserved fruits of any kind you have, and mould if desired.

FRUIT SYRUPS

N.B. If the prepared syrups referred to in some of the foregoing recipes cannot be got at the time required, recourse may be had to the syrup in recipe No. 87 for sweetening purposes.

WATER ICES

61. Water Ices made from Jams

150g (½ cup plus 2 tbsp) jam
570ml (2½ cups) cold water
juice of 1 lemon
food colouring

To the jam add cold water, the juice of 1 lemon; colour according to the fruit; pass through the tammy, and freeze. See note to No. 6.

62. Water Ices made from Fruit Syrups

285ml (1¼ cups) water
4 tbsp fruit syrup
food colouring

To the water add syrup. Colour according to the fruit, and freeze. See note to No. 8.

WATER AND PERFUMED ICES MADE FROM RIPE FRUITS, ETC

63. Apple Ice Water
(*Eau de Pommes*)

450g (1lb) apples
570ml (2½ cups) water
peel of ¼ lemon
2.5-cm (1-in) cinnamon stick
juice of 1 lemon
115g (½ cup) caster (granulated) sugar
570ml (2½ cups) water sweetened with 115g (½ cup) caster
(granulated) sugar

Put the apples to cook in the water, with a little lemon peel, cinnamon, and juice of 1 lemon and the sugar; when cooked, pass through the tammy, and add to the purée the sweetened water or 8 tbsp of syrup (No. 87). Freeze and serve in mould or roughly.

64. Apricot Ice Water
(*Eau d' Abricots*)

12 apricots
170g (¾ cup) sugar
570ml (2½ cups) water
yellow food colouring
570ml (2½ cups) water sweetened with 115g (½ cup) caster
(granulated) sugar or 160ml (⅔ cup) syrup (No. 87)

Take 12 apricots and stone them, break the stones and pound
the kernels; put the apricots to cook in a clean pan with the
sugar and water, and cook them till quite smooth; add a little
apricot yellow, pass through the tammy, and add this pulp to the
sweetened water, or use the syrup, and freeze.

65. Banana Ice Water
(*Eau de Bananes*)

6 ripe bananas
115g (½ cup) caster (granulated) sugar
570ml (2½ cups) water
juice of 2 oranges or lemons
¼ tsp banana essence, optional

Peel 6 ripe bananas, pound them, and add the sugar, water, and the juice of 2 oranges, or lemons if preferred, a little banana essence if you have it; pass through tammy, and freeze.

66. Bergamot Ice Water
(*Eau de Bergamote*)

570ml (2½ cups) lemon or orange ice water (Nos. 75 or 79)
60ml (¼ cup) brandy
6 drops orange essence

Prepare a lemon or orange ice water for this, add pale brandy and 6 drops of essence of orange (bergamot). Freeze dry.

67. Blackcurrant Ice Water
(*Eau de Cassis*)

900g (2lb) blackcurrants
285ml (1¼ cups) water
285mil (1¼ cups) fruit syrup

Boil the blackcurrants in the water. Sieve, mix with the fruit syrup and freeze.

68. Cedrat Ice Water
(*Eau de Cédrat*)

1l (5 cups) lemon ice water (No. 75, doubled)
50g (¼ cup) minced citron, or to taste

Prepare the lemon ice water, rub off the zest of 2 fine citron, add it to the lemon water, tammy or strain it, and freeze.

69. Cherry Ice Water
(*Eau de Cerises*)

900g (2lb) sour cherries
1l (5 cups) boiling water
280g (1¼ cups) sugar
red food colouring
2 tbsp kirsch

Stone the cherries, crack the stones and pound the kernels, pour the boiling water on the fruit and kernels and the sugar; colour with red food colouring and let stand till cold, then pass through the tammy, and add kirsch, and freeze.

70. Cranberry Ice Water
(*Eau de Cranberges*)

225g (2 cups) cranberries
280g (1¼ cups) sugar
285ml (1¼ cups) water
juice of 2 lemons
red food colouring
additional 570ml (2½ cups) water

Put the cranberries to cook with the sugar, and water; when cooked, add the juice of 2 lemons, a little red food colouring, and pass through the tammy. Add this pulp to the additional water, and freeze.

71. Damson Ice Water
(*Eau de Prunes de Damas*)

900g (1lb) damson plums

Stone the damsons and make in the same manner as cherry ice water (No. 69). Freeze either for fancy moulds or to serve rough.

72. Ginger Ice Water
(*Eau de Gingembre*)

225g (½lb) preserved ginger
1l (5 cups) orange ice water (No. 79, doubled)

Pound the preserved ginger, mix it with the orange ice water (No. 79); pass it through the tammy, and freeze. Either mould or serve rough.

73. Grape Ice Water (without grapes)
(*Eau de Grappes*)

570ml (2½ cups) lemon ice water (No. 75)
2 tbsp dried elderflower infused with 60ml (¼ cup)
boiling water
60ml (¼ cup) sherry

To the lemon ice water add the elderflower water and sherry. Freeze and mould or serve rough.

74. Jasmine Ice Water
(*Eau de Jasmin*)

Substitute 2 tbsp jasmine tea infused in
60ml (¼ cup) boiling water

This is made in the same way as bergamot ice water (No. 66),
only essence of jasmine (use jasmine tea infused in boiling
water) is used instead of bergamot. Freeze for moulding or to
serve rough.

75. Lemon Ice Water
(*Eau de Citron*)

570ml (2½ cups) boiling water
peel of 6 to 8 lemons
280g (1¼ cups) sugar
juice of 4 to 6 lemons
⅛ tsp lemon extract

Pour the boiling water on to the lemon peel and sugar; when cool, mix with the juice of the lemons; add the lemon extract; tammy or strain through sieve, and freeze for moulding or for serving in glasses.

76. Mille Fruits Ice Water
(*Eau de Mille Fruits*)

1l (5 cups) lemon ice water (No. 75, doubled)
225g (1 cup) diced assorted fruit

Prepare the lemon ice; add to it when partly frozen the mixed fruits cut in square pieces; any kind of fruit left from dessert will do for this ice. Serve in mould or rough.

77. Melon Ice Water
(*Eau de Melon*)

1 melon
285ml (1¼ cups) water
75g (⅓ cup) caster (granulated) sugar
juice of 2 oranges or lemons
2 tbsp curaçoa or maraschino
additional 570ml (2½ cups) water

Take off the skin of the ripe melon and pound the melon till smooth, then add the water, sugar, the juice of 2 oranges or lemons, and the curaçoa or maraschino; add this to the additional water, and freeze for moulding or to serve rough.

78. Mulberry Ice Water
(*Eau de Mûres*)

450g (1lb) mulberries
115g (½ cup) caster (granulated) sugar
red food colouring
juice of 1 lemon
570ml (2½ cups) cold water

Pick and then pound the mulberries; add to them the sugar, a little liquid red food colouring, juice of 1 lemon; pass through the tammy, then add to the cold water, and freeze. Serve as in previous recipes.

79. Orange Ice Water
(*Eau d'Oranges*)

Prepare this the same as for lemon ice water (No. 75), only use oranges instead of lemons.

80. Peach Ice Water
(*Eau de Péches*)

6 ripe peaches
570ml (2½ cups) water
115g (½ cup) caster (granulated) sugar
juice of 1 lemon
2 tbsp crème de noyeau
2 tbsp orange-flower water
red food colouring

Peel 6 good peaches and crack the stones, and remove the kernels, which must be pounded; put in a stew-pan with the water, sugar, and juice of 1 lemon; cook the fruit for 15 minutes, then tammy, and add the noyeau and orange-flower water, plus a little red food colouring. Freeze.

81. Pear Ice Water
(*Eau de Poires*)

6 ripe pears
850ml (3¾ cups) water
170g (¾ cup) sugar
peel of ¼ lemon
2.5-cm (1-in) cinnamon stick
red food colouring

Peel 6 good-sized pears and cut in slices, and put them to cook in the water with the sugar, a little lemon peel and cinnamon; add a little red food colouring when cooked; pass them through a tammy, and freeze.

82. Pineapple Ice Water
(*Eau d'Ananas*)

1 pineapple
850ml (3¾ cups) water
170g (¾ cup) sugar
juice of 2 lemons
juice of 1 orange
pineapple cut in fancy shapes, optional

Peel the pineapple and take out the core, put it to cook for 15 minutes, with the water, sugar, and the juice of 2 lemons and 1 orange, then pound; mix the liquor in which it was cooked with it and pass through the tammy, and freeze. A few pieces of the pineapple may be cut in rounds or dice shapes, and added to the frozen ice just before serving. Mould if wished.

83. Raspberry Ice Water
(*Eau de Framboises*)

This is prepared the same as for strawberry ice water (No. 86), only using raspberries instead of strawberries.

84. Redcurrant Ice Water
(*Eau de Groseilles*)

Proceed as for blackcurrant ice water (No. 67), only use redcurrants instead of black. Freeze, and mould if wished.

85. Rose Water Ice
(*Eau de Roses*)

225g (½lb) unsprayed rose petals
570ml (2½ cups) boiling water
115g (½ cup) caster (granulated) sugar
red food colouring

Take the fresh-gathered rose leaves, pour boiling water on them, with sugar, and keep closely covered up; then strain off and colour with a little liquid red food colouring, and freeze.

86. Strawberry Ice Water
(*Eau de Fraises*)

450g (1lb) strawberries
170g (¾ cup) caster (granulated) sugar
juice of 1 lemon
red food colouring
570ml (2½ cups) cold water

Put the strawberries in the mortar and pound them, then add the caster sugar, the juice of 1 lemon, a little liquid red food colouring; pass through the tammy, mix this to the cold water, and freeze. Serve as in previous recipes.

87. Syrup for Water Ices

675g (2¾ cups) caster (granulated) sugar
1.7l (7 cups) cold water

Put the sugar in a clean pan to boil with the cold water, keep well skimmed, reduce to half the quantity, and strain through the tammy or clean cloth. This will keep well. It may be used for sweetening the ices instead of the sugar.

SORBETS, ETC

The Italian word *sorbetto*, meaning sherbet, shows the origin of these dishes. Their general character is that of a water ice mixed or flavoured with wine or spirits. They are served before the roast in glasses or fancy cups, and generally just enough frozen to be piled up in the glass, or they may be moulded in little shapes and served with or without fruit. The following recipes will be sufficient for guidance, and they can be varied according to desire.

88. Sorbet of Peaches
(*Sorbet de Pêches à la Portugaise*)

6 ripe peaches
170g (¾ cup) caster (granulated) sugar
juice of 2 oranges or 12 grapes
570ml (2½ cups) cold water
6 drops red food colouring

¼ tsp yellow food colouring
2 tbsp kirsch
sliced peaches and chopped pistachios

Take 6 ripe peaches and peel them, and add to them the caster sugar, the juice of 2 oranges or 1 dozen grapes; crack the stones and pound the kernels and put to the fruit, and add to the cold water; add about 6 drops of liquid red food colouring and the apricot yellow, and tammy; then freeze, and when frozen add the kirsch, and serve with sliced fresh peaches and chopped pistachio nuts over.

89. Sorbet of Strawberries
(*Sorbet de Fraises*)

450g (1lb) strawberries
170g (¾ cup) caster (granulated) sugar
red food colouring
juice of 1 lemon
570ml (2½ cups) water
2 tbsp curaçoa or 1 tbsp rum or brandy
sliced strawberries tossed in caster (granulated) sugar and brandy

Take the strawberries, and add to them the caster sugar and a little red food colouring, the juice of 1 lemon; pass through the tammy, and to this add the water, and partly freeze; then add the curaçoa, and rum or brandy; continue the freezing, and serve in sorbet cups or glasses. If you have little strawberry moulds, you can put the sorbet in them, and freeze them for about half an hour. Serve with cut fresh fruits over, which have been flavoured by being tossed in a little brandy and caster sugar.

90. Sorbet of Apricots
(*Sorbet d'Abricots à la Moscovite*)

60g (⅓ cup plus 1 tsp) apricot jam
½ tsp yellow food colouring
570ml (2½ cups) cold water
2 tbsp maraschino
1 tbsp rum or brandy
diced preserved or fresh fruit, sprinkled with caster
(granulated) sugar
angelica

Take the apricot jam, apricot yellow food colour, and cold water, pass through the tammy and freeze; then add the maraschino and rum or brandy; freeze firm, and serve with square pieces of apricots, cherries, and angelica. In summertime fresh fruit can be used, when the fruit should be cut up and a little sugar sprinkled over it before serving. This is served in sorbet cups or glasses.

91. Roman Punch
(*Punch à la Romaine*)

1l (5 cups) water
560g (2½ cups) caster (granulated) sugar
peel of 3 lemons
juice of 4 to 6 lemons
60ml (¼ cup) dark rum

Boil the water, and add to it the sugar; when quite boiling, pour it on to the peel of 3 lemons and the juice of 4 to 6 lemons; cover over till cold, then strain through the tammy, and freeze; when partly frozen, add the Jamaica rum, and serve in sorbet cups or in glasses.

92. Another way

1l (5 cups) lemon ice water (No. 75, doubled)
5 egg whites, stiffly beaten
a pinch of salt
115g (½ cup) caster (granulated) sugar
2½ tbsp brandy
285ml (1¼ cups) champagne

Make the lemon ice water; when cold, have the whites of the eggs whipped stiff, with a tiny pinch of salt, then add the caster sugar, and partly freeze the lemon ice, and then mix to it the whipped egg, and continue freezing till smooth; when smooth, add the brandy and champagne; continue to freeze, and serve in sorbet cups or glasses.

93. American Sorbet
(*Sorbet à l'Americaine*)

Imitation glasses
Catawba wine or champagne
See Introduction, pp. 21–2.

Make some imitation glasses, by freezing water in tin moulds prepared for the purpose, and make a sorbet as above (No. 92), flavouring it with Catawba wine or champagne. Serve the sorbet in the imitation glasses. These imitation cups or glasses can be made transparent, marble-like, or coloured.

94. Rum Sorbet
(*Sorbet au Rhum*)

prepared lemon water ice (No. 75)
60ml (¼ cup) dark rum per 570ml (2½ cups)

Prepare a lemon water ice, and when nearly frozen, flavour with Jamaica rum.

MOUSSES

Mousses are frozen without stirring.

These make excellent sweets, and are very much liked on account of their lightness. They are served as an *entremets*, sometimes for dessert. The following recipes will show the method of making them.

95. Coffee Mousse
(Mousse au Café)

9 or 10 egg yolks
4 egg whites
3 or 4 tbsp caster (granulated) sugar
3 tbsp coffee
¼ tsp coffee extract
150g (½ cup plus 2 tbsp) whipped cream (90ml / ⅓ cup plus 2 tsp unwhipped)

Whip the yolks of eggs, whites, caster sugar, coffee and extract over boiling water till warm, then take off and whip till cold, and add whipped cream; whip these well together. Put in a mould, and freeze for about 2½ hours. To turn out, dip the mould in cold water. Serve with dish-paper, or napkin or dish.

96. Strawberry Mousse
(*Mousse aux Fraises*)

12 egg yolks

4 or 5 egg whites

115g (½ cup) caster (granulated) sugar

150g (½ cup plus 2 tbsp) strawberries, pulped to a purée

1 tsp vanilla essence

red food colouring

285g (1¼ cups) whipped cream (175ml / ¾ cup unwhipped)

Put the raw yolks of eggs into a pan, with the whites of eggs, caster sugar, the pulp of the fresh strawberries, vanilla essence and a little red food colouring to colour; whip till warm over boiling water, then remove and whip till cold and thick, then add the whipped cream; whip these together, and put into any fancy mould, and freeze for about 2½ hours. Turn out and dish same as No. 95.

97. Maraschino Mousse
(*Mousse au Marasquin*)

2½ tbsp maraschino

This is made in the same manner as the vanilla mousse below, but instead of the vanilla essence add maraschino for flavour.

98. Vanilla Mousse
(*Mousse à la Vanille*)

10 egg yolks

3 or 4 egg whites

75g (¼ cup) caster (granulated) sugar

2 tsp vanilla essence

150g (½ cup plus 2 tbsp) whipped cream (90ml / ⅓ cup plus 2 tsp unwhipped)

Put the yolks of eggs into a pan, with the whites and caster sugar, essence of vanilla; whip this over boiling water till warm, then remove the pan from the fire and continue whipping till cold and stiff, then add to this the whipped cream; put into any kind of mould, and freeze for 2½ hours. Turn out same as No. 95.

ICED SOUFFLÉS

Soufflés are not stirred while freezing.

These very much resemble the mousses, but as they are served in dishes or cases, and the mousses are moulded, a slight difference is required in the ingredients and in the time for freezing. The following recipes will be sufficient for guidance.

99. Coffee Soufflé
(*Soufflé au Café*)

10 egg yolks

5 egg whites

80ml (⅓ cup) very strong coffee

115g (½ cup) caster (granulated) sugar

285g (1¼ cups) whipped cream (175ml / ¾ cup unwhipped)

baking parchment

Take a soufflé dish and surround it inside with parchment standing about 5 centimetres (2 inches) above the top, and put it into the freezer to get cold.

Take and whip over boiling water the raw yolks of eggs, the whites, the very strong coffee and the caster sugar, until like a thick batter, then remove and continue the whipping on ice till the mixture is cold; to this quantity add whipped cream; pour this into the mould, letting it rise above the mould to near the top of the paper. Freeze for 2½ hours, and serve in the mould with a napkin around or in a silver soufflé dish. Of course these quantities may be proportionately increased or diminished to suit the size of the mould.

100. Vanilla Soufflé
(*Soufflé à la Vanille*)

8 egg yolks
4 egg whites
3½ tbsp caster (granulated) sugar
1 tsp vanilla essence
80g (⅓ cup) whipped cream (50ml / a scant ¼ cup
unwhipped), sweetened with ½ tsp caster (granulated) sugar

baking parchment

Prepare the soufflé dish as in No. 99. Take the raw yolks of eggs, the whites, caster sugar and a little vanilla essence; whip over boiling water, take off when rather warm and whip till cold and stiff, then add about the lightly sweetened whipped cream. Finish as in No. 99.

101. Strawberry Soufflé
(*Soufflé de Fraises*)

480g (2 cups) whipped cream
(285ml / 3⅓ cups unwhipped)

Prepare a mousse as in No. 96, using about half as much more cream whipped, and finish as in last recipe.

102. Coffee Soufflés in cases
(*Petits Soufflés au Café*)

paper soufflé cases: See Introduction, p. 19.
baking parchment and sealing wax
Coffee soufflé (No. 99)

Take the little paper soufflé cases and fasten round each a strip of parchment, fixing it with sealing wax; let the paper stand about 4cm (1½ inches) above the top of the case. Prepare the soufflé mixture as in No. 99; fill the case and over it to nearly the edge of the paper surrounding it, and place them in the freezer for 1½ hours; when frozen sufficiently remove the paper and serve.

Any soufflé can be served in a similar manner. Fruit and vanilla soufflés would be improved in appearance by sprinkling a little coloured sugar over them.

DRESSED ICES, ETC

It is impossible to give more than a few under this head, as the variety that can be made with the various moulds, flavours, etc., is almost unlimited; but the mixtures which can be used will be found among the foregoing recipes, and some designs in colours are given in the book as examples.

103. Strawberry and Vanilla Bombe
(*Bombe à la Vanille et Fraises*)

Strawberry ice water (No. 86)

FOR THE VANILLA CUSTARD:
285ml (1¼ cups) milk or single (light) cream
1 vanilla pod
3 tbsp caster (granulated) sugar
4 egg yolks
additional 3 tbsp caster (granulated) sugar
6 drops brandy

Prepare the strawberry ice water and freeze it quite dry; have the vanilla custard prepared with the milk or cream boiled with a stick of vanilla and caster sugar, and when flavoured sufficiently pour on to the raw yolks of eggs and thicken over the fire; then tammy and freeze, and add, when partly frozen, more caster sugar and 6 drops of brandy; line a bombe mould with the strawberry water ice and fill up the centre with the vanilla custard, and freeze for 2 hours. To turn out, dip the mould in cold water and serve on a napkin.

104. Bombe with Fruits
(*Bombe aux Fruits*)

Chocolate cream ice (No. 21)
Vanilla cream ice (No. 58)
2 tbsp kirsch
285g (1¼ cups) whipped cream (175ml / ¾ cup unwhipped)
candied fruit soaked in syrup, to taste

Take a bombe mould and line it with chocolate ice cream, then fill up the centre with vanilla cream ice mixed with the kirsch, whipped cream, and cut candied fruits which have been soaked in syrup. Freeze for 2 hours, turn out as in last recipe, and serve on a dish-paper or napkin.

105. Sovereign Bombe
(*Bombe à la Souveranne*)

Almond cream ice (No. 10)
Coffee mousse (No. 95)
a flat, round sponge cake, plus extra for decoration

Line the sides and top of a bombe with a layer of almond cream ice, and fill up the interior with a tea mousse (see recipe No. 95 for coffee mousse).

Freeze for 2 to 3 hours according to size of mould; serve it on a border of sponge cake, and garnish the dish with the same cake cut in small fancy shapes.

106. Plain Ice Pudding
(*Pouding Glacé*)

850ml (3¾ cups) single (light) cream
285ml (1¼ cups) milk
10 egg yolks
a pinch of mixed spice
280g (1¼ cups) caster (granulated) sugar
1 vanilla pod

2½ tbsp brandy

2 tbsp kirsch

To the cream add the milk; put it in a stew-pan with the raw yolks of eggs, a pinch of mixed spice, the caster sugar, the split pod of vanilla; stir this over the fire till it thickens and presents a creamy appearance on the wooden spoon; then tammy, and when cool add the brandy and kirsch; freeze, and put into any mould and freeze for 2 hours.

107. Nesselrode Pudding
(*Pouding à la Nesselrode*)

This is prepared the same as No. 106, with the addition of various cut fruits being mixed with the custard before putting into the mould. If fresh or dried fruits are used, they should be soaked in a little liqueur or spirit and sprinkled with sugar before being mixed. Fruits preserved in syrups may simply be cut up and mixed.

108. Sauce for above

A sauce is sometimes served with the Nesselrode pudding, and is made by preparing a rich custard (No. 1) and flavouring it with vanilla or maraschino. Keep it on the ice and serve as cold as possible.

109. Chateaubriand Bombe (*Bombe à la Chateaubriand*)

FOR THE VANILLA CUSTARD:
850ml (3¾ cups) milk or single (light) cream
150g (⅔ cup) caster (granulated) sugar
1 vanilla pod
10 egg yolks

PART ONE:
½ tsp vanilla essence
4 tsp orange-flower water
green food colouring
80g (a scant ⅓ cup) whipped cream (50ml / a scant ¼ cup
unwhipped) sweetened with ½ tsp caster (granulated) sugar

PART TWO:

75g (3oz) almonds, blanched

1 tbsp butter

2 tbsp caster (granulated) sugar

To prepare the vanilla custard, put the milk to boil with the caster sugar and vanilla split in shreds; let this come to the boil, cool slightly and remain on the side of the stove in the pan covered up for about 15 minutes, not boiling; then mix it on to the raw yolks of eggs and thicken over the fire. Divide the custard into two parts; put to one part a few drops of essence of vanilla and the orange-flower water, and colour it with apple green to the colour of pistachio, and tammy; it is ready then to freeze, and when partly frozen add half the sweetened whipped cream. Put the blanched almonds in a sauté pan, with the fresh butter and caster sugar; make these quite a deep brown over the fire, and then pound them quickly in the mortar till smooth; mix them with the other part of vanilla custard, and pass through the tammy; when frozen, add cream as to the other part of the custard, and freeze. Arrange the 2 ices thus prepared in a fancy mould in layers, or the mould can be entirely lined with the green, and the centre filled with the brown ice. Freeze for 2 hours.

110. Ginger Bombe
(*Bombe au Gingembre*)

285ml (1¼ cups) milk
peel of 1 lemon
75g (⅓ cup) caster (granulated) sugar
3 or 4 egg yolks
¼ tsp ginger
juice of 1 lemon
6 drops vanilla essence
285g (1¼ cups) whipped cream (175ml / ¾ cup unwhipped)
sweetened with ½ tsp caster (granulated) sugar
75g (⅓ cup) diced crystallized ginger

Prepare a custard made with the milk, boiled with the lemon peel and caster sugar; when the milk boils, mix it on to the raw yolks of eggs and as much ginger as will cover a threepenny piece, thicken over the fire and tammy, then add the juice of 1 lemon and 6 drops of vanilla essence, and when cool freeze; when partly frozen, add the sweetened whipped cream; line the bombe mould with this, and have the preserved ginger cut in dice and put in the centre; fill up with more custard, and freeze for 1½ hours.

Turn out and serve on a napkin or dish-paper.

111. Bartlett Pudding
(*Pouding à la Bartlett*)

6 ripe Bartlett pears
570ml (2½ cups) water
juice of 2 lemons
170g (¾ cup) caster (granulated) sugar
55g (¼ cup) diced candied pineapple
55g (¼ cup) diced glacé (candied) cherries
285ml (1¼ cups) double (heavy) cream
75g (¼ cup) caster (granulated) sugar caramelized with 60ml
(¼ cup) water
3 egg whites, stiffly beaten

FOR THE SAUCE:
1 additional egg white
2½ tbsp whipped cream (1½ tbsp unwhipped)
1 tbsp maraschino
the reserved pear syrup

Peel and cut up in thin slices 6 ripe Bartlett pears, cook them
in water with the juice of 2 lemons and the sugar; when tender,
drain them through a sieve and pass the fruit through a tammy
or fine hair sieve; mix with this the pineapple cut fine, dried
cherries, and the thick cream, and freeze; when partly frozen,

have ready to mix with it the whipped whites of 3 eggs, to which have been added sugar, cooked to caramel. When cooked add the boiling caramel to the stiffly beaten egg whites, continuing to beat them, and add to the frozen mixture, and continue the freezing, and mould. The syrup from the pears must be used for the sauce for serving round the pudding. Prepare it as follows: Whip the white of 1 egg and mix it with the whipped cream and maraschino; add the pear syrup and cool over ice. When the pudding is turned out, pour the sauce over it and serve.

112. Plombière of Strawberries
(*Plombière de Fraises*)

570ml (2½ cups) double (heavy) cream
10 egg yolks
⅛ tsp mixed spice
280g (1¼ cups) caster (granulated) sugar
570ml (2½ cups) strawberries pulped to a purée
red food colouring

½ tsp vanilla

2 tbsp brandy

Put the cream in a pan with the raw yolks of the eggs, a tiny pinch of mixed spice, and the caster sugar; stir together on the stove, and when nearly boiling add to it the pulp of fresh strawberries which has been passed through the tammy cloth, a little red food colouring, half a teaspoonful of essence of vanilla, and the brandy; freeze and mould, and leave in the freezer for 2 hours; then dip in cold water, and turn out on a napkin or dish-paper.

113. Muscovite of Oranges
(*Moscovite d'Oranges*)

280g (1¼ cups) caster (granulated) sugar

peel of 8 to 10 oranges

½ tbsp powdered gelatine soaked 5 minutes in 60ml (¼ cup) cold orange juice

540ml (2¼ cups) boiling water

yellow food colouring

juice of 8 to 10 oranges

½ tbsp maraschino or brandy

whipped cream sweetened and flavoured to taste, optional

Put the sugar with the peel of the oranges and the gelatine, and pour over them the boiling water and a little saffron yellow; let this stand till cool, then mix the juice of the oranges to it and strain through the tammy, and add a little maraschino or brandy to flavour. Pour into a mould and freeze for about 2 hours; turn out as in the last recipe. This can be served with whipped cream sweetened and flavoured.

114. Muscovite of Strawberries
(*Moscovite de Fraises*)

450g (2 cups) strawberries, pulped to a purée
170g (¾ cup) caster (granulated) sugar
540ml (2¼ cups) warm water with ½ tbsp powdered gelatine
juice of 1 lemon
red food colouring
½ tbsp crème de noyeau
single (light) cream and strawberries mixed with syrup,
optional

Pass the strawberries through the tammy, add the caster sugar, warm water in which has been dissolved the leaf gelatine, the juice of 1 lemon, a little red food colouring, and a little noyeau; pour into a mould, and put to freeze for about 2 hours. To turn it out, put the mould into cold water for a few seconds. This can be served with cream or fresh strawberries, mixed with a little syrup.

115. Little Soufflés of Cheese
(*Petits Soufflés de Fromage Glacés*)

55g (¼ cup) grated Parmesan cheese
3 tbsp grated Gruyère cheese
a speck of cayenne pepper
285g (1¼ cups) whipped cream (175ml / ¾ cup unwhipped)
150g (⅔ cup) aspic jelly (p. 112)
browned bread crumbs, for serving

Mix together the grated Parmesan cheese, Gruyère, cayenne, whipped cream, and aspic jelly. Mix and fill up the cases (see No. 102), and freeze for 1 hour. Serve with browned bread-crumbs on the top.

116. Iced Spinach à la Crème
(*Epinards Glacées à la Crème*)

2 or 3 handfuls fresh spinach
285ml (1¼ cups) milk
3 or 4 egg yolks
green food colouring
2 tsp caster (granulated) sugar
80g (⅓ cup) whipped cream (50ml / a scant ¼ cup
unwhipped) sweetened with ½ tsp caster (granulated) sugar
2 pinches of salt

FOR THE BORDER:
570ml (2½ cups) single (light) cream
2 tsp caster (granulated) sugar
2 tsp orange-flower water
¼ tsp vanilla essence

Put the spinach in cold water with salt; let it come to the boil; strain off and press the water from it. Boil the milk and stir it on to the yolks of eggs, and put it on the stove again to thicken but don't let it boil; add a little apple green to colour it, and add the caster sugar and another pinch of salt; mix with the spinach, pass through the tammy, and freeze; add, when partly frozen, sweetened whipped cream. Freeze dry and mould in a Neapolitan box [a loaf pan will do] and freeze for about 1½ hours; then cut out in cutlet shapes. Dish on a border of iced cream; for this use cream, caster sugar, and orange-flower water, and a few drops of vanilla. Freeze dry and mould in a border mould.

117. Soufflés of Curry à la Ripon
(*Petits Soufflés de Kari à la Ripon*)

55g (¼ cup) butter
2 onions, sliced
2 tart apples, sliced
a sprig of thyme
2 bay leaves
a sprig of parsley
55g (¼ cup) grated fresh coconut
6 almonds, blanched
1 sole or flounder

½ tsp curry powder

½ tsp curry paste

½ tsp tamarind

salt

juice of 1 lemon

milk, to cover

yellow food colouring

150g (½ cup plus 2 tbsp) whipped cream (90ml / ⅓ cup plus 2 tsp unwhipped)

aspic jelly (see over)

cooked prawns (large shrimp), to garnish

Fry in the butter 2 onions sliced, 2 sour apples, the sprig of thyme, 2 bay leaves, sprig of parsley, coconut and 6 almonds blanched; to this add a raw or cooked sole or whiting. Fry all until a good golden colour, then add half a teaspoonful of curry powder, half a teaspoonful of curry paste, half a teaspoonful of tamarind, a little salt, and juice of 1 lemon; cover then with milk and cook till tender, add a little saffron yellow to colour. Take the meat from the fish bone and pound, and pass through a tammy cloth; add this purée to the whipped cream with aspic; whip well together. Freeze in cases (see No. 102) for 1½ hours. When serving, garnish with prawns.

Aspic Jelly for No. 117

50g (¼ cup) powdered gelatine soaked for 5 minutes in 240ml
(1 cup) cold water

1l (5 cups) boiling water

20 peppercorns

juice of 1 lemon

2 tsp salt

120ml (½ cup) vinegar

1 onion

½ tsp dried tarragon

2 bay leaves

whites and shells of 2 eggs

Dissolve the gelatine in boiling water over the fire with 20 peppercorns, the juice of a lemon, the salt, vinegar, 1 onion, a little fresh tarragon (or a tablespoonful of tarragon vinegar), and a couple of bay leaves. Clear with the whites and shells of 2 eggs (see p.115); strain off when it boils.

GLOSSARY

Almonds, sweet and bitter: Sweet almonds are the variety generally available in markets. The intensely flavoured bitter almond, still used in Europe, may be replaced by a discreet quantity of almond extract (⅛ to ¼ teaspoon). Imitation bitter-almond flavouring, imported from Germany, can be found in specialty food shops.

Almond essence: Almond extract.

Angelica is a biennial plant whose hollow green stalks are candied, sliced, and cut into ornamental shapes to decorate food. It is also used to flavour liqueurs.

Banana essence is still available.

Bergamot essence: Mrs. Marshall probably means essence of the bergamot orange, since she uses it in an orange water ice. There is also a bergamot pear, and the herb bergamot (*Monarda didyma*), which is better known as Oswego tea.

Biscuit: Any plain, unsweetened biscuit can be used, or the cook may wish to try the following recipe from Mrs. Beeton, *The Book of Household Management* (1861): 'Crisp Biscuits. Ingredients. 450g (1lb) of flour, the yolk of 1 egg, milk. *Mode*. Mix the flour and the yolk of the egg with sufficient milk to make the whole into a very stiff paste; beat it well, and knead it until it is perfectly smooth. Roll the paste out *very thin*; with a round cutter shape it into small biscuits, and bake them a nice brown in a slow oven from 12 to 18 minutes. Time. 12 to 18 minutes. *Average cost*, 4d. *Seasonable* at any time.'

'Break, or crack, the stones': This was a common technique used to extract the flavour from fruit pits. Mrs. Marshall uses it with peaches, apricots, cherries, and plums. You may substitute ⅛ to ¼ teaspoon of almond extract, or ½ tablespoon of crème de noyeau, or a suitable fruit brandy.

Cedrat: The citrus fruit of the citron tree, shaped like a lemon but as large as a grapefruit. Only the rind is used, and it is always candied. The cook may substitute 55g (¼ cup) finely chopped citron, or any other proportion suitable to the needs of a particular occasion.

Cherry, Kentish: This is the red morello, a juicy sour cooking cherry.

'*Clear with the whites and shells of two eggs*': Crush the shells, beat the whites until foamy, and add both whites and shells to the cooled liquid mixture. Then heat slowly until it has just begun to simmer. Hold it at this temperature for five minutes, and then strain it through a dampened cheesecloth. If the aspic is not entirely clear, the process may be repeated. However, since in recipes 115 and 117 it is subsequently mixed with other ingredients, crystal clarity is unnecessary.

Coconut: If coconuts are not available, you may make a mildly-coconut-flavoured custard by warming 375g (2½ cups) of unsweetened coconut in 570ml (2½ cups) each of milk and single (light) cream gently for half an hour. Keep covered; do not let the mixture simmer or boil. You may wish to reinforce the coconut effect by adding a tablespoon of the grated coconut to the ice-cream mixture before freezing. Do not substitute sweetened coconut. It contains far too much sugar, which can prevent your ice cream from freezing.

Colourings: Mrs.. Marshall uses colour to excess, by twenty-first-century standards. In some cases food colourings may be needed, but usually two or three drops will suffice. As air is churned into a mixture during the freezing process, its colour will become lighter. The cautious cook will err on the side of delicacy.

Crack the stones: See break the stones.

Cream: Use single (light or medium) cream unless an especially
   rich ice cream is desired. Whipped cream is measured after
   whipping; 175ml (¾ cup) of unwhipped cream will usually
   yield about 285ml (1¼ cups) of whipped cream.

Curry paste: When I tested Soufflés of Curry à la Ripon, I omit-
   ted the curry paste and increased the curry powder proportionately. To satisfy the reader's curiosity, however, here is a
   recipe from a contemporary source. It should be remembered
   that English 'corn' is American 'wheat.' Both sweet oil and
   mustard oil may be found in stores specializing in Indian
   foods.
      From T. F. Garrett's *Encyclopaedia of Practical Cookery*
   (189–): 'Put into a mortar ½ lb. of roasted coriander-seeds,
   1 oz. of roasted cumin-seeds, 2 oz. each of black pepper, dry
   chillies, dry tumeric, and mustard-seeds, 1 oz. each of dry
   ginger and garlic, and 4 oz. each of sugar, salt, and roasted
   corn (gram däl), and pound well, pour in sufficient white-
   wine vinegar to bring the mixture to the consistence of jelly.
   Warm some sweet-oil in a pan, and as soon as it commences
   to bubble, drop in the mixture and fry until it is reduced to
   a paste. When this is cold, put it in bottles, cork them, and
   keep in a dry place until wanted for use. Mustard-oil may

be substituted for the sweet-oil, but on no account must any water be allowed to get into the paste, or it will be spoilt.'

Damsons: Small tart purple cooking plums.

Filberts: Domestic hazelnuts. In Mrs.. Marshall's day the best came from Spain and were therefore called Spanish nuts.

Ginger: Mrs.. Marshall uses several forms, all of which are still available. Preserved ginger comes in two forms: in a syrup and crystallized. In testing these recipes I have used the latter. Ginger brandy and a variety of ginger wine, made with green ginger and currants, are both available today.

Lemon essence: Lemon extract.

Liqueurs: Kirsch, maraschino and crème de noyeau are all man-ufactured today. Do not attempt to substitute maraschino syrup for the real, colourless liqueur. Noyeau, made from peach kernels, has a character all its own; if unobtainable, ⅛ teaspoon of almond extract or a few drops of imitation bit-ter-almond flavouring may be substituted.

Mixed spice: From T. F. Garrett's *Encyclopaedia of Practical Cook-ery* (189): 'Pound 2 oz. [50g] each of allspice, cloves, and cinnamon, ½ oz. [15g] each of nutmeg and ginger, and 2 oz. [50g] of coriander-seeds. When they are well powdered they must be kept in a well-stoppered bottle.'

Paper soufflé cases: See Introduction, p. 19.

Ratafia biscuits: When I tested Mrs.. Marshall's recipe for ratafia cream ice, I first used good-quality modern macaroons from a bakery. It was the only occasion on which I had a total failure; the ice cream was too sweet to freeze solid. Then I made it with Mrs.. Beeton's ratafia biscuits, halving the recipe, and it turned out very nicely. I used sweet almonds, almond extract, a few drops of imitation bitter-almond flavouring, 170g (¾ cup) of caster (granulated) sugar, and 2 egg whites. In place of a biscuit syringe, the cook may use a pastry bag and tube with a nozzle measuring about ½ centimetre (¼ inch), or the batter may simply be dropped from a teaspoon. For cartridge paper substitute parchment paper.

From Mrs.. Beeton, *The Book of Household Management* (1861): 'Ingredients. ½ lb. [225g] of sweet almonds, ¼ lb. [110g] of bitter ones, ¾ lb. [350g] of sifted loaf sugar, the whites of 4 eggs. *Mode*. Blanch, skin, and dry the almonds, and pound them in a mortar with the white of an egg; stir in the sugar, and gradually add the remaining whites of eggs, taking care that they are very thoroughly whisked. Drop the mixture through a small biscuit-syringe on to cartridge paper, and bake the cakes from 10 to 12 minutes in a rather quicker oven [150°C/300°F/gas mark 2] than for macaroons. A very small quantity should be dropped on the paper to form one cake, as, when baked, the ratafias should be about the size of a large button. Time. 10 to 12 minutes. Average cost, 1s. 8d. per lb.'

Sugar: For loaf and lump sugar, use modern caster (granulated) sugar, except that if you are extracting flavour oils from candied citron rind, you will still need to use lump sugar.

Tammy cloth: Agnes Marshall uses a tammy, or fine strainer, for two distinct purposes. The first is to cool her custard promptly after it has thickened; we may achieve the same purpose by putting the saucepan in cold water (see pp. 16–17). Secondly, the tammy is used to keep lumps out of a purée and to ensure a uniform consistency. By the late nineteenth century, a sieve was more commonly used than a cloth, as the following definition in T. F. Garrett's *Encyclopaedia of Practical Cookery* indicates: 'Tammy: A kind of woollen cloth . . . used for straining fruit syrups, liquid jellies, etc. The French cook uses the term 'tamis' for a fine meshed sieve of any kind, the word having originated from the cloth used at one time to form the sieve or strainer.'

LIST OF RECIPES